C000182530

EASTBOURNE THEN & NOW

IN COLOUR

JOHN SURTEES & NICHOLAS TAYLOR

First published in 2012

The History Press
The Mill, Brimscombe Port
Stroud, Gloucestershire, GL5 2QG
www.thehistorypress.co.uk

© John Surtees & Nick Taylor 2012

The right of John Surtees & Nick Taylor to be identified as the Authors of this work has been asserted in accordance with the Copyrights, Designs and Patents Act 1988.

All rights reserved. No part of this book may be reprinted or reproduced or utilised in any form or by any electronic, mechanical or other means, now known or hereafter invented, including photocopying and recording, or in any information storage or retrieval system, without the permission in writing from the Publishers.
British Library Cataloguing in Publication Data.
A catalogue record for this book is available from the British Library.

ISBN 978 0 7524 8576 8

Typesetting and origination by The History Press
Printed in India.

CONTENTS

ACKNOWLEDGEMENTS

To our families for their encouragement, and our thanks also go to: Stanley Apps, Betty and Arthur Cobb, Ann and Alan Caffyn, Mavis Clack, John V. Claremont, Bob Elliston, Ian Ford, Lawrence Ford, Vera Hodsoll, Graham Household, George Humphrey, Roger and Jean Gordon, Kevin Gordon, Clive Griggs, Derek Keay, W.H. Kefford, Marie Lewis, Lou McMahon, Pauline Markquick, Rosemary and John Milton, Frances Muncey, Dr J.D. O'Connor, Michael and Tim Partridge, Jack Putland, Harold D. Spears, John and Irene Stevens, Pat and Lawrence Stevens, Joan and Ken Thurman, and Catherine Tonge.

Also to Beckett Publications; the British Library; Caffyn's plc Publicity Department; Channel Photography; the Eastbourne Local History Society; and Judges Postcards.

Any relevant individual or organisation which inadvertently has not been acknowledged is asked to accept the authors' apologies.

ABOUT THE AUTHORS

John Surtees was born in the north of England and after graduation worked there and in Edinburgh and London until appointed to a post in the Eastbourne district. History was a great interest outside his profession and he was the Medical Archivist to the Eastbourne hospitals for many years. A vice-president of the Eastbourne Local History Society, he is a local broadcaster on radio and TV and writes articles and gives talks and leads walks on historical aspects of Sussex. He is the author (three jointly) of twelve books. His special interests include Beachy Head, Downland villages, Dr John Bodkin Adams, Eastbourne hospices and hospitals, the Eastbourne Salvation Army riots, Medical Services in the Korean War and old laboratory equipment.

Raised on the Sussex coast from 1960 and educated locally before reading chemistry at Imperial College, Nicholas Taylor, a Medical Photographer of over thirty years' experience, twenty at Eastbourne DGH, has contributed numerous photographs to medical journals and textbooks as well as local history books.

INTRODUCTION

Eastbourne has a significant history before sea bathing, the main reason for its development, appeared in the mid-1700s. There is evidence of Stone Age, Bronze Age and Iron Age habitation. There was a Roman villa just by the pier and the Saxons are represented by grave goods on Ocklynge hill, but such examples do not lend themselves to 'Then' pictures.

It was decided, therefore, to use a selection of black and white pictures from our *Images of England – Eastbourne* book and contrast them with colour images of the same view today. There are, interestingly, a few examples that show almost no change over the last century and, inevitably, it was not always feasible to use the precise 'Then' viewpoint for a few of our 'Now' pictures.

Hence we present all aspects of life in the town: the seafront blessed by nature and mankind, the Old Town with so many hidden places worth discovering, the Victorian developments so well supported and yet benignly controlled by the two main land-owning families in the town (the Dukes of Devonshire and the Davies Gilberts) – and we even attempt to contrast a few 1960s 'Then' with 2012s 'Now'. Quite a few examples are from the Second World War because they do make dramatic contrasts of scene, but also bring to mind the town's front-line wartime experience: it was the most frequently bombed town on the South Coast.

Eastbourne has a lot going for it. Since the royal princes stayed in 1780 it was always popular as a resort and it has kept abreast with the times, but without tarnishing a lovely seafront or its Carpet Gardens, the parades and safe bathing beaches. It has a popular new marina, unexplored old corners, the South Downs are on its doorstep, with the Weald and forests nearby, there are good schools and theatres, it is healthy (we're told), it hardly ever snows and (if you'll believe us) the sun always shines.

We hope you enjoy our pictures and that they give you reasons to ponder the changes in Eastbourne and the progress of life in general.

John Surtees and Nicholas Taylor, 2012

DEVONSHIRE PLACE

WHEN THE 7TH Duke of Devonshire 'got rid of' James Berry (1796-1877) as his surveyor and architect he appointed Henry Currey (1820-1900) in his place. Currey lived in London, but he came from an Eastbourne family. He fashioned two Eastbourne plans, in 1859 (central town) and 1872 (Meads), which with the Duke's money and the support of George Ambrose Wallis, the Duke's surveyor, transformed Eastbourne.

The 1859 plan changed the centre of the town and nearby seafront, introducing spacious thoroughfares. Devonshire Place, clearly named after the Duke, is considered by many to be one of the most glorious byways in Britain with its views out to sea and to the gentle Downs inland.

Currey was famously surveyor and architect to St Thomas' Hospital, London, and went on to build the Eastbourne College Chapel, the Queen's Hotel and the Devonshire Park Theatre among many other commissions in Eastbourne and elsewhere.

DEVONSHIRE PLACE TODAY retains much of its magnificence, its broad roadway functioning as a dual carriageway with central car-parking thrown in. In the distance, the war memorial of 1920 has replaced the Princess Alice tree, but the background of the Downs, where visible, hasn't changed and the lines of trees have not been entirely lost. Thanks to artificial hip and knee joints bath chairs have now gone completely, although the horse droppings have merely been supplanted by the smells of oil and petrol.

The grand houses are now mainly flats, but a welcome addition has been the seated figure of William Cavendish, the 7th Duke, looking out to sea and presiding over the town he created. Paid for by public subscription – a testament to the 'worthy life' of the 7th Duke – this fine bronze memorial, on a granite base, was unveiled on 17 August 1901 by the Marquess of Abergavenny. The edifice was the work of Sir William Goscombe John.

THE PRINCESS ALICE TREE SQUARE

SOUTH STREET WITH the broach spire of St Saviour's church and, on the right, the Princess Alice tree. The foundation stone of the church was laid in 1865.

The tree commemorated the most successful visit of Queen Victoria's second daughter in the autumn of 1878. Princess Alice, aged just thirty-five, died shortly afterwards of diphtheria, caught when nursing her children.

The church was built with £20,000 donated by the maker of Whelpton's Pills, one of the conditions being that his son be appointed the vicar. The Duke of Devonshire gave the land (it had been a turnip field) and £1,000 towards the cost of the spire. When, in 1872, the weathervane was finally placed on the top by the said vicar the congregation sang below, but the vane fell off shortly afterwards and was not replaced.

George Whelpton was one of the Victorian 'patent medicine millionaires', along with other purveyors of 'useless restoratives' such as Beecham's Pills and Holloway's Powders. In those days the average person couldn't afford a doctor and, apart from the few People's Dispensaries, most folk passed their short lives without ever seeing one.

UNVEILED IN 1920, the Angel of Victory commemorates the 1,000 Eastbourne residents who died in the First World War and the many who gave their lives in the Second, including 174 civilians killed in the bombing of the town.

The spire of St Saviour's church (now St Saviour and St Peter's) is untouched; fortunately, the only bomb to hit the church failed to explode. It was always the fashionable church, where the mayors and top businessmen of the town worshipped, but was regarded by many as 'rather high', no doubt in line with its 54-metre spire – the tallest in the town.

The shop frontages on the right are almost untouched – although H.R. Browne's, the dispensing chemists on the corner, who were there from mid-Victorian time (and were the shop of choice of the infamous Dr John Bodkin Adams, suspected of murdering as many as 160 of his patients) closed in 1976. If you look on the step at the entrance to the furnishing shop of today you will see 'H.R. Browne' picked out in the tiles.

MEADS LOOKING EAST FROM BEACHY HEAD

ALL SAINTS' CONVALESCENT Hospital is middle left of this image, towards the edge of the photograph, and St Luke's Children's Hospital is in the centre, just behind the gabled private houses in the foreground. The parades and Western Lawns are towards the right, with the pier and town in the middle distance.

Any resort boasting of its health-giving qualities had to have a convalescent hospital to demonstrate the benefits of its healing airs, so when, in 1867, Mother Harriet and a group of Anglican nursing nuns came to Eastbourne they were greeted enthusiastically. They built

All Saints' Convalescent Hospital, which opened in 1869, joined in 1874 by a finely proportioned chapel by Henry Woodyer. The hospital thrived for many years.

From the 1830s coastguard cottages were situated near the seafront at Meads, but in 1890 they were replaced by St Luke's, a children's convalescent hospital associated with All Saints', and a memorial to Mother Harriet, who had died in 1887.

THE ALL SAINTS' red-brick buildings were taken over by the NHS in 1960 after the nuns left in 1959. The hospital was finally sold in 2004 for redevelopment and by 2008 there were fifty flats in the old hospital and another fifty in the grounds.

St Luke's never fully reopened after the Second World War and was sold to be developed as a block of fashionable flats, Dolphin Court, completed in 1965. The building is easily recognisable in the centre by the three white covers on the roof.

The gabled house in front looks unchanged from the previous view apart from the trees that have grown up around it.

Towards the middle distance is South Cliff Tower, another block of flats. They are an eminently desirable residence, but their building in 1966 raised an outcry in the town, with 'carbuncle' being amongst the mildest of the critical responses; one result was that the mayor, who had owned the land, was defeated at the next election.

GRAND PARADE AND CARPET GARDENS

THE GRAND PARADE and Carpet Gardens looking west, *c*.1900. From 1851, when the Grand Parade was built, there were always gardens in front, in the early days merely a low hedge and lawns. In the 1880s the council took over their maintenance and introduced floral designs, some of which were based on the patterns seen in the Persian carpets fashionable in the day. Names such as 'Flowering Beds' were used to describe them, but the name 'Carpet Gardens' took root and is now well-known. This design does indeed bear a resemblance to a carpet pattern.

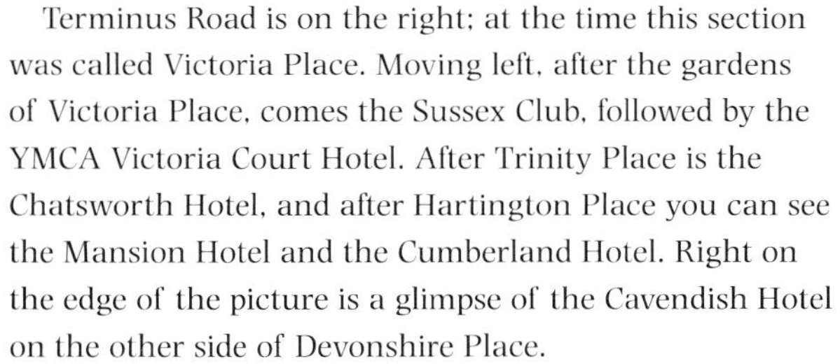

Terminus Road is on the right; at the time this section was called Victoria Place. Moving left, after the gardens of Victoria Place, comes the Sussex Club, followed by the YMCA Victoria Court Hotel. After Trinity Place is the Chatsworth Hotel, and after Hartington Place you can see the Mansion Hotel and the Cumberland Hotel. Right on the edge of the picture is a glimpse of the Cavendish Hotel on the other side of Devonshire Place.

THE CARPET GARDENS looked more like flowering beds when this early spring photograph was taken in 2012. On the other side of the Grand Parade traffic, the gardens of Victoria Place now form part of Terminus Road and have been built over with shops. Harry Ramsden's fish and chip shop is at the edge of the Grand Parade; the covenants forbid the opening of shops on the parade itself.

The Sussex Club buildings, which housed the public library after the main library was bombed in 1943, have been replaced by Clive Court, a block of flats, and the old Victoria Court Hotel, now Sovereign Court, is yet more flats. The Cavendish Hotel is again just visible on the extreme left.

EASTBOURNE SEAFRONT

BEACHY HEAD IS at the top of the picture. The pier is near the centre. Meads is the uppermost, built-up area, with the Seaside area towards the lower part of the town. The Crumbles, at the lower edge, was a bank of shingle thrown up over the years to the east of Eastbourne, gradually blocking an inlet that ran inland as far as Polegate in Roman times. This explains why the Roman fort of Pevensey, originally built to assist the Roman fleet in their efforts to contain Saxon pirates, is situated a few miles inland today. The town has been extended since the 1930s but, along the front, the most striking change has been the conversion of the treeless shingle bank of the Crumbles into a popular marina and residential area.

THIS PHOTOGRAPH EXTENDS a little further eastward than the 1930s one shown on the opposite page. While the town has extended in all directions, perhaps the greatest change is the construction of Sovereign Harbour seen at the lower part of this picture at Eastbourne's eastern end.

The shingle-extracting work for building materials ceased in the 1980s and the first boats went through the locks in 1993. The granite breakwaters leading to the 1,000-berth marina can clearly be seen on the left, leading to the Outer Harbour where Eastbourne's lifeboat is now moored. The locks are situated between the Outer and Inner Harbours where moorings are visible. The development of the Sovereign Harbour has progressed even more in recent years to provide a corner for the fishing boats, all the repair and replacement facilities a yachtsman might require, plus a variety of residences, shops and restaurants at the waterside. Just to the right are department stores and a duplex cinema. *(Courtesy of Channel Photography)*

ST PETER'S CHURCH, MEADS

ST PETER'S STOOD at the junction of Meads and Granville Roads. It began in 1878 as a chapel of rest for St Saviour's on a site behind where the Town Hall is now. In 1893 this land was gifted by the 8th Duke of Devonshire, along with £500 towards the building's construction. The foundation stone was laid by the Duchess of Devonshire on 26 September 1894, and consecrated on St Peter's Day 1896 by Dr E.R. Wilberforce, the Bishop of Chichester.

The lady chapel was added in 1900 and the vestry and sacristy in 1902. The architects were none other than Henry and Percival Currey and – surprise, surprise – the likely builder was William Lumb Wallis, the brother of George Ambrose Wallis, former mayor and the Duke's surveyor.

ALTHOUGH ST PETER'S church was a listed building it was declared redundant in 1971 and knocked down over the next year. The benefices of St Saviour's and St Peter's were reunited in 1971. The reredos screen at St Peter's was saved and is now in St Saviour's and St Peter's church, South Street.

The Granville Road site was sold for sheltered housing and Redman King House replaced the church.

A SPORTING SCENE

EASTERN SEAFRONT SPORTING scene, *c.*1900. This picture was taken looking north-east of the Redoubt Fortress with Royal Parade houses on the left. The tennis courts and bowling greens can be seen, along with the thatched Pavilion of the day. This is not the site of the Tea Pavilion of today, which is on the south-east side of the Redoubt in front of the old Colonnade and bandstand.

THE GROWTH OF some of the trees makes it difficult to obtain exactly the same view, but the terrace of gabled houses in Royal Parade is much the same and the activities generally unchanged: bowling greens and, in the distance, tennis courts are still in evidence.

In the distance there are also more buildings: the Fisherman's Club, for example, and newer entertainments such as Treasure Island.

EASTBOURNE'S FIRST THEATRE, SOUTH STREET

EASTBOURNE'S FIRST THEATRE, South Street, *c.*1880. It was built for the Fisher family in 1798 to entertain the increasing number of visitors and the militia sent into the area to defend England against invasion from Napoleon. Audience numbers dropped after the troops

left and before the railway came to the town in 1849, so in 1838 the building was converted into a carpenter's shop by the Haines family, 'Builders and Upholsterers'.

Later the firm went into the funeral undertaking business and moved to the opposite side of South Street, after which the old theatre building was demolished; the Royal Hippodrome and the Devonshire Park theatres had been built by that point.

QUITE A DIFFERENT scene; now a more congested South Street, this view is from close to the Dewdrop Inn. The area is noted not only for its congested roadways, but for the many shops that line the pavements. There are book shops (although not as many as there were), brokers, pubs, nightclubs, art shops (hardly any left) and many others – and quite a few funeral directors, including Haine and Sons Ltd.

BEACHY HEAD

ON TOP OF Beachy Head looking east, *c*.1905. From the left is a wall that ran round the signalman's or watchman's cottage; behind that is the Beachy Head Hotel. At the centre, near the skyline, are the coastguards' cottages. To the right is the signalman's lookout, and just nearer to the viewer the semaphore pole he used for messages. The signalman was employed by Lloyd's of London to report on vessels laden with tea from China and wool from Australia working up the Channel. His report would be transmitted by semaphore to London where the news could affect the price of these commodities and influence the insurance markets.

When wireless telegraphy came into use, the work was transferred to the coastguard station in 1904. Having said that, on a clear day the signalman could get a message to London in about a quarter of an hour, which is around the time it takes a certain person to find his mobile.

NOT ONLY HAS the wall around the signalman's cottage gone, but the cottage itself has been flattened and assiduously removed. The Beachy Head Hotel is a newer one, but on the same site. The coastguards' cottages survived the Second World War: however, they were victims of the peace (or more so, the Cold War) when they were removed in 1950 in the course of building an underground radar station which many described as a nuclear bunker. Not an inappropriate description, for it is about the size of the Grand Hotel, but buried under Beachy Head chalk. The station/bunker was declared redundant in 1957. There were plans to open it up as part of the Eastbourne holiday experience, but although in good condition the developers got cold feet in the depression of 1991-3 and it was closed up.

The semaphore mast has long gone and the signalman's lookout was reduced to a twelve-brick-course observation post, which you can see on the skyline. The telescope has been removed, so it is just a seat these days although emblazoned with many plaques recording associated events. Over the century the cliffs have receded, but not by much.

THE SPENCER ROAD BOMBING

A TRAGIC WARTIME event occurred in Spencer Road on Saturday, 3 April 1943. This image shows all that remained of a surface air-raid shelter in Spencer Road after it took a direct hit from a 250kg (500lb) bomb dropped by one of ten Me 109s and FW 190s German fighter-bombers just before noon, contributing to the greatest number of civilian fatalities (thirty-three) in a single raid on Eastbourne. These simple 9in-thick concrete-roof and brickwork

shelters were designed as blast, splinter and debris protection for people caught out of doors during an air raid, but not to withstand a direct hit and, as can be imagined from the scene, all those sheltering inside were killed.

In one of the enigmas of life and death, William Edmonds, a pharmacist at Temple's chemist in South Street (the road straight ahead), usually didn't go into a shelter for these 'Hit-and-Run' raids; if the occasion demanded, he would go down into the shop's cellar. On this day, however, a twelve-year-old boy, Peter Horton, a friend of Mr Edmonds' young daughters, had just walked into the shop so the two rushed over to the Spencer Road shelter, where both died.

THE SHOPS AHEAD in South Street are largely unchanged – apart from nameplates.

A block of flats, College Court, has replaced the damaged South Street building alongside the site of the shelter. The name refers to the one-time presence of Eastbourne College nearby. When the college opened in 1867 its fourteen pupils were housed in temporary quarters in a private house at 1 Spencer Road as recorded on a plaque outside. The college staff and pupils transferred to College House, Blackwater Road, in 1871.

GRAND PARADE

GRAND PARADE. THIS was the 7th Duke of Devonshire's first Eastbourne development. This drawing, looking west, is of the projected development by James Berry. Berry was the Duke's architect at the time. This image dates from 1851, before the pier and parades, but the concept of gardens in front of the buildings is shown in the sketch. The accommodation was let out to families and to visitors, but because of the inadequate infrastructure – the roads around were not made up – business was slow and many of the builders went bust despite the support of the Duke.

THIS VIEW, TAKEN from the pier entrance, shows that the Grand Parade has hardly changed. Nowadays the whole of the building is devoted to the Burlington Hotel at 11-33 and, nearest, the Claremont Hotel at 5-10.

During the years that No. 22 was privately owned, it was the site of some skulduggery. In 1860 Thomas Hopley, who ran a small school there, was charged with the murder of a pupil by administering corporal punishment. He was sentenced to four years' imprisonment. Incredibly, there were letters in the local press suggesting that going soft on administering the cane was the cause of many of the world's woes.

Then, in 1918, George Hayes, the pier manager, lodged here. At the age of forty-one he received his call-up papers for the army. He attempted to escape conscription by passing himself off as a fifty-year-old (i.e. not subject to conscription) with the same name. His bluff was called and he was charged with 'impersonation with the aim of avoiding call-up', this at a time when such an action was considered despicable. However, the Chief Constable of Eastbourne spoke up for him in mitigation and he received a light sentence. There was uproar, and the Chief Constable was eventually forced to resign.

THE TECHNICAL INSTITUTE

THE TECHNICAL INSTITUTE, *c*.1910. This is looking south-west from near the station, with Grove Road to the left and Old Orchard Road to the right. With the town's rapid expansion, by the end of the 1800s Eastbourne was badly in need of a technical college and a public library. The Duke of Devonshire had gifted a suitable site in 1899, and in August 1904 the Technical Institute was opened by the Duchess of Devonshire thanks to a £10,000 donation from Andrew Carnegie, the

oil and steel millionaire and philanthropist, who visited the town the next year and was made a freeman of the borough.

The ground floor was given over to a museum and a library. For the first few years you had to tell the librarian what book you wanted and it would then be brought to you. The first floor held the Technical Institute and Continuation School, with the School of Art on the top floor.

THE TECHNICAL INSTITUTE was bombed on Friday, 4 June 1943. At 11.30 a.m. some eighteen FW 190 fighter-bombers, flying low over the sea, swept up over the Beachy Head cliffs and dived onto the town causing extensive damage from Paradise Drive to Seaside. Along with the Technical Institute bombing, the nearby MacFisheries in Grove Road was hit, resulting in library books and fish being found as far away as the Avenue, and giving rise to the comment that there was food for both 'the body and the mind' in the area that day.

The library was at a number of temporary sites until, on 6 April 1964, it returned to this site in a sparkling new building. The schools moved into the premises of The Grange, a school in St Anne's Road that had been evacuated, and stayed there until 1997. In that year all the facilities transferred to new premises on Cross Levels Way which, together with Lewes College, now form Sussex Downs College.

EASTBOURNE MATERNITY HOSPITAL

EASTBOURNE MATERNITY HOSPITAL, *c*.1975. This view looks across Upperton Road from the Hartfield Road entrance. Upperton, at No. 9 Upperton Road, was one of a line of large houses built in the late 1880s. In 1915 it was taken over as a Red Cross hospital to help cope with the number of casualties in the war. It had seventy beds, all in two-bedded wards named after the heroes and heroines of the day such as Jellicoe and Cavell. The medical officers gave their services free and, apart from two paid nurses, all the other helpers were voluntary. After the war, at the instigation of Dr W.G. Willoughby, the medical officer of health, it was bought for use as a maternity home by the borough council – one for married mothers only.

With extensions it provided twenty-five beds. The mothers paid two guineas a week and stayed on average seventeen and a half days, enjoying the rest before returning to their large

families: remember that this was in the days before the contraceptive pill, washing machines, tumble dryers and vacuum cleaners.

IN 1949, WHEN the maternity home had 550 deliveries, there were also 201 home births, 64 in nursing homes and 2 in hospitals. Gradually, with improvements in antibiotics, anaesthetics, Caesarean deliveries and blood transfusions, mothers (especially for first babies) were safer in hospitals, and such facilities were easily available. By 1971, out of 1,422 births in Eastbourne, 933 were in hospital (most staying only for a day or two), some 400 at the maternity home and just 3 home deliveries.

Over 20,000 babies had been born in the maternity home before closure in 1976, on the opening of the District General Hospital along King's Drive, to where maternity services were transferred. The ex-maternity home – or No. 9, as it was called – became an NHS administration block and, in 1977, an Ambulance Control Centre opened in the grounds. In the late 1990s the site was vacated and sold for development. The old maternity home was demolished and, in 2000, Marlborough Court, a block of flats with a warden and a resident's dining room, opened.

ORCHESTRAL MUSIC ON THE SEAFRONT

THE 'BIRDCAGE' BANDSTAND on Grand Parade in 1926. Before the First World War, Eastbourne had two orchestras, a municipal one and the Duke of Devonshire's. After the war, the Duke's was subsumed into the municipal orchestra, with Captain Henry Amers as the conductor from 1920 to 1936. Amers inaugurated an annual music festival in 1923, which was the start of a fine tradition of seafront orchestral and military band music. Amers was always smartly attired, leading to whispers – but no more – that he wore a corset.

THE 3,000-SEAT central bandstand built at a cost of £29,000 to replace the Birdcage. It was first used in 1935, with the official opening on 5 August of that year by Lord Leconfield. Over the years it has hosted many popular concerts and continues the tradition of military music – although this could be under threat. A perennial favourite is the Boxing Day Dance to a veteran pop band.

In the arcade there is a memorial to a *Titanic* victim who had played in the local orchestras.

It is now a listed building, but needs more than a lick of paint to bring it up to the standards required.

THE LAMB INN

LOOKING DOWN THE High Street (on the right) towards the town, with Ocklynge Road entering on the left, *c.*1900. The Lamb Inn, Old Town, is the oldest pub in Eastbourne, although probably not quite as old as claimed. It started out as a pilgrims' rest stop and became the centre of Eastbourne life as it was situated at the crossroads next to the parish church, with the Gildredge Manor House nearby in the Goffs. In the cellars there is a ceiling boss of 1300s design, but whether it was fashioned at that time is doubtful – 'fashions' often took a century or two to reach Sussex. There is little doubt, however, that the oft-made assertion of tunnels running from the cellars to the church and to Pilgrims, a house on the other side of the High Street, is ill-founded.

In Georgian times, when the building shown here was last altered, rendering was often used to reduce damp and to obscure half-timbering, which was then considered 'old hat'. The signs also show that in around 1900 the pub was keeping up with the times by catering for cyclists.

IN 1912 A runaway horse damaged the rendering and, as half-timbering was once again all the rage, most of the plaster was removed to display the timbers.

This spot, once a crossroads of the Saxon settlement, remained the centre of activity of Bourne, as it was known in Saxon times, although most archaeological finds, mainly grave goods, have been found on the Ocklynge ridge. The road to the left, Ocklynge Road, once the main road for the London stagecoaches, was cut off from the High Street and Church Street in the 1990s.

BATTLE OF BRITAIN DAY FOR EASTBOURNE

NUMBER 85 LATIMER Road was destroyed after a bomb exploded in the back garden on Sunday evening, 15 September 1940.

The date is now celebrated as Battle of Britain Day, but it was one of the lightest days over that autumn of action for Eastbourne. Only the previous day there had been six raids of varying intensity, with seven deaths and fifty-six injured.

The weird effects of the blast are well shown here: the back wall of the bedroom has been blown out, but the bed, dressing table and ewer remain in place (although balanced precariously).

COMPLETE REPAIR OF the house at the side and back, and a bay window added upstairs at some time, means that if you didn't know it was No. 85 you would hardly believe that the back wall of the house had been blown apart on that 1940 evening.

The bombing was one of the 'incidents' recorded when, at around 7 p.m., three German planes strafed the area from the seafront to Astaire Avenue with seventeen high-explosive bombs, an oil bomb (which probably didn't explode, as was the rule) and hundreds of 2kg Thermite incendiary bombs. Thankfully, no casualties resulted.

HOLYWELL RETREAT

HOLYWELL RETREAT AROUND the early 1900s. The name Holywell is now bestowed on what was the Gore Chalkpit at the seaward end of Meads, but Holywell was originally an area further west along the front where fresh water springs emerged at the scarf line.

In the 1800s there was a tiny fishing community there, but in 1896 the Eastbourne Water Co., in trouble for over-extracting at the Bedfordwell site and looking for extra sources of supply, installed a pump at Holywell and the springs dried up. To avoid contamination the fishing community were moved to the eastern side of the town. Even the pub at the chalk quarry closed and its licence was transferred to The Pilot in Meads Street.

IN 1904-5 THE Corporation arranged for the chalk quarry (which had exported chalk for many years) to be laid out by unemployed workmen as an Italianate garden. The cost of the work was £400, which the Corporation had to borrow. The Tea Garden, part of which can be seen below on a lower parade, was created in 1921-3.

By the 1930s the Holywell area was another attractive section of the Eastbourne front and in March 1935, as part of the preparations for their Silver Jubilee, King George V and Queen Mary came to the town and visited No. 2 chalet, near the Holywell Café.

More recently some of the footpaths round the gardens, which have needed work on them to make them safe, have been closed for safety reasons.

EASTBOURNE FRONT AND THE WISH TOWER

EASTBOURNE FRONT LOOKING west towards the Wish Tower, *c.*1895. The Wish Tower stands out on the skyline and on the left is Hounsom's temporary ticket office for booking bathing-machine hire. Mixed bathing too – what next?

The Wish Tower was No. 73 of the Martello Towers built along the South Coast between 1805 and 1812, as part of the defences against Napoleon. This one is called Wish Tower because it was situated on an outcrop surrounded by marshy land (called a wish in these parts).

They were adapted from a defensive tower in Corsica which held out against an English attack. Squat, circular, brick-built with thick walls (thicker on the side facing the sea), their armament was a 24-pounder gun, or larger. Along Pevensey Bay, a likely landing place, they were arranged so that each gave covering fire to adjacent towers. Many have been eroded by the sea; others were destroyed by artillery practice or demolished for development. One was destroyed by enemy action in the Second World War. In England they ran from Suffolk to Seaford, but there were Martello Towers in Ireland, the Channel Islands, Canada and South Africa.

THIS PART OF the front has changed little. The temporary huts have altered: some have become chalets, but the general picture is much as it was over a century before.

The Wish Tower has also changed little, although the moat has been filled in. By 1818 it was in the care of a Royal Artillery corporal and a sergeant of the Royal Sappers and Miners. It was later occupied by the coast blockade, the coastguard (1831-1851) and the Royal Artillery (*c.*1861). The Wish Tower was leased to the Corporation in 1884 and became a private museum shortly afterwards. Used again for anti-invasion defences in 1940, with two 6in guns mounted in front, demolition was considered after the war, until it was listed as a scheduled monument. The present gun, a 68-pounder with a range of nearly 2 miles, is not original, having been cast in 1858.

SPLASH POINT

SPLASH POINT, JUST east of the pier, 1905. Behind the spray is the Queen's Hotel. Opened in 1880, and popular today, the hotel was designed by the 7th Duke of Devonshire's architect, Henry Currey, known for many works in Eastbourne and elsewhere.

As far as Eastbourne was concerned, the working class was divided into those in service, usually with low wages, and those who depended on tourism, where the work was seasonal. The Queen's Hotel was planned to delineate clearly the hovels of the working-class artisan in the east of the town from the folk who lived in mansions to the west. It was said that, pre-1939, no lady would venture east of the Queen's Hotel.

Although James Berry, the Duke's architect in the early 1850s, did make an effort to protect the seafront, the first serious attempt to control the sea was to construct an embankment, opened in 1884, which ran from near the pier to the Redoubt.

SEA CONTROL IS in better shape these days, with more shingle and groynes and a spray-protective brick wall along the seafront road.

The Queen's Hotel is much the same, although the upper two rows of balconies have been removed. The hotel was in danger of losing its chimney pots, but after complaints most have been kept.

There remain differences between the west and east sides of the town, but not sufficient to stop people from the west going into the east, or vice-versa. Pre-1939, it was also said that no lady carried a handbag – implying that you had servants for that stuff (and would expect to be given credit in shops) – but now handbags are universally carried by women, east and west, although there is a pecking order: the more expensive, the better.

CHARLESTON ROAD

FLYING BOMB DAMAGE, Charleston Road, June 1944. London was the main target for the pilotless flying bombs (or V1s, more usually called doodle-bugs), and the later V2 rockets. The name 'doodle-bug' came from the 'phut-phut' noise made by the paraffin engine, which was just like the sound made by a model car of the day.

Eastbourne only suffered from malfunctioning or damaged ones, so just fifteen V1s landed in the town and just one V2. There were fatalities among service personnel in the area, but no one died among the civilian population from these weapons.

In the early evening of 18 June 1944 a V1, probably hit by anti-aircraft fire, fell in Old Town, destroying seven houses and severely damaging others in Charleston, Milton and Mountney Roads. Forty-one civilians were injured, including a teenage woman who lost the sight in one eye.

A MUCH MORE settled domestic scene of suburbia. Whilst there was no sign of cars in the 1940s, today you can hardly take a photograph without including just a few. There is a mixture of repaired houses and new houses, none too dissimilar to the damaged houses that were repaired.

On 7 August 1944, around midnight, another doodle-bug crashed in nearby Baldwin Avenue, demolishing several houses and causing widespread damage – including St Elisabeth's church, which never truly recovered. In this instance the V1 was on fire as it crossed the coast, but as the engine kept running it didn't dive to the ground as usual, but slowly lost height. If you were underneath one it's not easy to decide which type of descent you would prefer.

THE SOUTH LYNN SCHOOL THAT WAS

'A LARGE SEMI-CASTELLATED brick building on the very crest of the hill, almost the first conspicuous sight of all Eastbourne as one comes in by rail': such was an 1897 view of the school.

South Lynn was a boys' school from 1880 to 1914, one of the many in Eastbourne in the late 1880s. During the First World War it was taken over for a Royal Naval Air Service Officers' Mess and over the next decade it was home to no less than three different girls' schools.

Captain Lawrence Oates (1880-1912) of Antarctic fame, who deliberately walked out into a blizzard to enhance his comrades' chances of survival, was a pupil at the boys' school before going on to Eton. There was a plaque to his memory in St Anne's church in Upperton Gardens, where he worshipped. Sadly, however, the church was bombed and set on fire in August 1942, and was later demolished.

THIS IS PART of South Lynn Drive, a fourteen-house development around a quiet cul-de-sac which replaced South Lynn School in the 1930s. The architect was P.D. Stonham (1877-1942). Numbers 4, 6, 8 and 10 overlie parts of the old school.

In Eastbourne of the late 1800s and early 1900s, education was the most important business after tourism. Around 1890 there were some eighty private schools in the town: some families moved to the town to avail themselves of the tremendous choice of schooling available. Some catered for the children of families working in the colonies. There would also be many small, often temporary, 'crammers'. The number of boys' and girls' schools was fairly equal.

These schools were not available, of course, for the vast majority of Eastbourne children, who were instead crammed into a few church schools, because Eastbourne Council wanted to keep the rates down and were one of only two authorities not to have a School Board. This state of affairs persisted until the Education Act of 1902, after which the council had to provide state-funded education for all its children, greeted with cries of, 'It'll be spend, spend, spend now' by the irate ratepayers.

THE OLD INFIRMARY

PART OF THE union workhouse: the old infirmary, built in 1889. The infirmary block looking south towards Vicarage Road. This wardblock replaced a one-storey flint building used to segregate infectious workhouse inmates in times before the 'fever hospital' was opened – the first formal attempt to separate fit and ill inmates. When the workhouse became St Mary's Hospital in 1930 this block housed medical and surgical wards, a 'lean-to' operating theatre until 1958 and, from 1967, a built-on ITU. After the inception of the NHS in 1948 the nearest two wards to the camera were named Berwick and Dicker, and the far two Alfriston and Cuckmere. Latterly, a physiotherapy department was added.

On the extreme left is the flat roof of the mortuary, whilst in the background was the eye clinic, later the occupational therapy department. The far houses are in Vicarage Road.

On the right foreground is a surface air-raid shelter from the Second World War, afterwards used as a Red Cross patients' library store for many years. The windows were installed during this era.

WITH THE EXCEPTION of the old 'sergeant-major's house' and the casual ward alongside Church Street, which were converted into flats, all the old buildings, comprising cavalry barracks, workhouse and hospital, were demolished in 1990.

This view is from the same spot in 2012, looking towards the houses in Vicarage Road along part of Letheren Place, a pleasant development put up in 1991-2. The site was named 'Letheren Place' after Miss Mary Letheren, a dedicated matron of the hospital from 1924 to 1948 who strove, with Dr Herbert McAleenan and Dr W.G. Willoughby, the medical officer of health, to bring the care at the workhouse, later hospital, up to the standards of the day.

The old hospital had a happy and devoted workforce, but all realised that the ancient fabric could not be moulded anymore when striving towards an ideal modern hospital. In 1989 the last of the services moved into the new District General Hospital on King's Drive. The staff raised sufficient funds to install a blue plaque, which can be seen on an outside wall from Church Street, commemorating nearly 200 years service to the town as cavalry barracks, workhouse and hospital.

THE BEACHY HEAD HOTEL

A POPULAR SPOT for a cup of tea in the 1930s. An inn nestling just behind the peak of the Downs on Beachy Head has been in existence for over 130 years and was originally called the Queen's Hotel. It was so popular that for many years it was licensed to stay open an extra hour on Sunday mornings and it was a meeting place for many, including the East Sussex Hounds' hunt. Rupert Brooke (1887-1915), the poet and icon of his age – 'And is there honey still for tea?' – stayed there in 1911. Like so many of his generation he perished in the First World War, dying from an infected insect bite while on his way to the Dardanelles.

The hotel suffered from a fire in the 1920s, but although the occasional incendiary and high-explosive bomb dropped during the Second World War it escaped severe damage. Just after the war, however, it was described as 'little more than a collection of shacks ... the fare was an unending supply of mince followed by bread and butter pud., with no choice, of course.'

Incredibly, the hotel did not have a piped water supply, even after the farms around were supplied in the 1930s. The hotel relied on rainwater tanks in the roof so, unsurprisingly, with water over a quarter of a mile away, it burnt down again in April 1966 and yet again in December 1994. Thankfully, however, there were no fatalities. Without delay, Whitbread's built an enlarged Brewer's Fayre, along with a countryside centre. Now it is a Vintage Inn.

About the same time, the police and coastguard radio mast (which can be seen over the hotel roof) and the rescue and recovery equipment for any falls at Beachy Head were moved inland, from across the road to alongside the hotel. Later the Samaritans moved their telephone box too: this allowed anyone in a distressed state of mind to contact the organisation. It has been used on several occasions.

BELLE TOUT LIGHTHOUSE

BELLE TOUT LIGHTHOUSE in the early 1900s and in 1945. Attempts to provide a light at Beachy Head to warn shipping had been made since the 1690s and in the early 1700s a local clergyman, Jonathan Darby, excavated a refuge in the cliffs from where he shone a light on stormy nights. The lighthouse finally came about as a result of the stranding of the *Thames*,

an East Indiaman, on Eastbourne's beach in 1822. The light became a tourist attraction, but otherwise it wasn't a success: although visible from 23 miles away on a clear night, on a misty night the light – which was 280ft high – tended to flash uselessly above the gloom. It was decommissioned in 1902 and for a short while it was used as a tearoom. Then it was bought for £1,500 by Sir James Purves-Stewart, a distinguished neurologist, in 1923. He installed a generator, added a top floor and entertained King George V and Queen Mary there in March 1935. During the war it was damaged – not by enemy action, but during artillery practice.

The site was known as 'Bel Tout' until the Victorians decided that applying the name of the Celtic god of war to such a charming spot was improper. Belle appeared from around 1840. 'Tout', pronounced 'toot', is also not French: it was a Saxon name for a look-out.

AFTER POCKETING £5,000 in war-damage compensation, in 1948 Sir James gave the lighthouse to the County Borough of Eastbourne – who clearly had no idea what to do with it. In 1956 Dr Edward Cullinan leased the building and by 1960 had made it sound. He died in 1962 and after his widow, Dorothea, sold the lease in 1980, the old lighthouse changed hands on numerous occasions.

In 1986 it was bought and upgraded, at a cost of £250,000, by the BBC for use as a location for a television series, *Life and Loves of a She-Devil*, starring Patricia Hodge and Dennis Waterman. Part of the contract stipulated that the building had to be returned to the same state as before once filming ended – a pity, for some of the changes had been improvements. In June 1988, Paul Foulkes, the lease holder, had the lantern room restored. It became a handsome summer lounge.

In 1994 the old lighthouse, now a Grade II listed building, was up for sale. The asking price was £350,000. In March 1999, the lighthouse was moved 50ft back on a set of greased runners – a two-day procedure – to save it from falling into the sea. Later bought by David Shaw, the old lighthouse had a £1 million makeover and is now in use as a popular top-grade B & B and tearooms.

CAFFYN'S GARAGE

CAFFYN'S GARAGE, MARINE Parade, 1904. In 1856 William Caffyn was apprenticed to his uncle Ebenezer Morris to learn the trade of 'ironmonger, tinman and brazier'. He opened his first shop in Meads Road as a gas and hot-water fitter in May 1865.

The first motor car was seen on Eastbourne's roads in May 1896, and in 1900 Harry Caffyn was asked to store a car in his electrical shop at No. 12, The Colonnade. Further requests – for no hotels had garages – convinced William's sons, Percy and Harry, that the future lay in cars, although as Percy explained, 'We didn't know what a garage was: we called it a coach house'. They opened this garage in 1902 and by 1929 Caffyn's were selling over 1,000 cars annually. In 1977 they acquired the Mercedes-Benz and Fiat franchises and in spite of many changes the company continues to flourish.

THE AREA AROUND Caffyn's garage received more than its fair share of bombs; nearby Bourne Street was known as 'bomb alley'. Almost inevitably, therefore, the garage in Colonnade Gardens was largely destroyed after a direct hit by a 500kg bomb on 6 June 1943.

This is the area today. A Tesco Express store is now on the site of the old garage. Many of the walls of the adjoining block were strengthened by wall supports during repairs.

A most bizarre episode of the countless Eastbourne Blitz events happened at a house in Old Town. The couple there had a metal Morrison table shelter in the living room into which they crawled at the start of an air raid. When the house was hit, and collapsed all around them, they were, therefore, kept safe in the shelter, and there awaited rescue. As was usual, the couple had an open fire in the living room. On that particular evening, however, they noticed that it was becoming warmer and warmer in the room, and realised – to their horror – that embers from the coal fire had set the debris alight. For a moment it looked as though they were going to be cooked – but suddenly, with a crack, the cistern on the roof split and water cascaded down to put all the fires out.

SUMMERDOWN CONVALESCENT CAMP

SUMMERDOWN CONVALESCENT CAMP, *c*.1916. Summerdown Camp was started up in 1915 to help wounded or ill soldiers back to fitness so that they could return to the front. At any one time there could be over 3,000 troops there – one of the largest such camps in Europe – and it is estimated that over 200,000 troops passed through the camp between 1915 and 1920, 90 per cent of whom went back to the various fronts.

The soldiers wore a distinctive uniform of white shirt, red tie and blue jacket and trousers, and were affectionately called 'the Blue Boys' by the people of Eastbourne. The men did not like the outfit because it stood out so much – but then that was the point, as it enabled the police and army 'red caps', as the military police were called, to identify anyone out of bounds.

The troops watched films on a Sunday, which wasn't allowed in the town, and also made their own entertainment. It was whispered that if you were sufficiently talented to hold your place in the variety company (Knuts Kamp Komedy Kompany) or the camp band you tended to have a more prolonged recovery period than was medically justified.

THE SUMMERDOWN CAMP site has been comprehensively developed since 1920. This is the view of one of the new roads, Old Camp Road, which runs just south of the centre of the old camp.

The outline of the camp's central road can be discerned from the air just to the north of Old Camp Road. Asphalt paths and the occasional concrete slab have been found buried in certain gardens. A number of the huts, which were auctioned off smartly after 1918, were to be found around the town and in neighbouring villages, although they are now coming to the end of their days as scout huts or village halls.

THE SALVATION ARMY

THE SALVATION ARMY plays away, on the beach by the Grand Parade. The Salvation Army first came to Eastbourne in 1890 and opened their citadel in Langney Road. Initially the organisation was welcomed, but some residents were irritated when the band broke an 1885 Eastbourne Improvement Act which forbade playing and marching on a Sunday. There was also some reaction against strangers coming into the county and attempting to change the set ways.

Discussions took place in the council chamber, with the mayor showing firmly against such behaviour on the Sabbath. Attempts to stop the band led to skirmishes. These were mainly led by louts, and encouraged by publicans worried by the possibility of stricter licensing laws coming into force. The culmination came on 19 July 1891 with the arrest of members of the Salvation Army Camberwell Band who had come to lend support to their fellow bandsmen and women. When some were sent to prison, most people thought matters were getting a bit out of hand. The next year the Salvation Army successfully promoted a Bill in Parliament to change the law on Sunday playing.

THERE IS LITTLE architectural change in the backcloth of the Burlington Hotel, although the brickwork lavatories and offices in front have been extended, and the shingle is noticeably more extensive. The Salvation Army continues to be active in the town, with the citadel as its headquarters. The band plays on Sundays, but usually by the pier or along Grand Parade – 'bringing the church to the holidaymakers', as they say.

CAVENDISH PLACE

CAVENDISH PLACE, AT the junction with Tideswell Road, looking north. Saturday, 28 September 1940 witnessed examples of exceptional gallantry and courage. Four bombs hit houses and shops at Tideswell Road, Bourne Street and Cavendish Place, where eight people were trapped in cellars.

Surgeon Mr Lawrence Snowball said later, 'Five were released by the rescue services, but a seventeen-year-old Hankham girl, I still recall her name – Miss Peggy Harland – was pinned by a steel girder across her ankles.

'She was in great pain and unable to move, yet she kept up her spirits – and those of the rescuers who were toiling to free her – despite an unexploded bomb nearby and the need for the constant pumping of water, which was leaking from a fractured water main nearby.

'After 24 hours, it was apparent that she could not be released – we hadn't today's heavy lifting gear – so Dr Roy Barron and myself crawled to her: he to give the anaesthetic and me to amputate both legs. Sadly, Miss Harland died in hospital two days later.'

She was posthumously awarded the Girl Guides Gilt Cross and fourteen gallantry awards were made to the rescuers.

LOOKING NORTH FROM Cavendish Place to Tideswell Road. The style and the clean brick of the block of flats on the right shows evidence of a new build, and the loss of rendering on the shops and houses on the far side of Tideswell Road shows where repairs had been made, along with some rebuilding.

This was in the most bombed area in the town and many streets had hardly a house standing at the end of the war. Thornton Court, in nearby Bourne Street, was built in 1952 on the site of 139 destroyed or severely damaged properties and has a wall plaque reading '...erected by Eastbourne Corporation as a tribute to the fortitude shown by the inhabitants during the air raids.' The siren went 1,346 times. There were also 353 local warnings and about 500 incidents (the so-called Hit-and-Run Raids) which struck without warning. It was only thanks to evacuation, the town's residents falling at one time from 50,000 to nearly 10,000, that the casualties were not heavier.

THE EASTBOURNE TUBERCULOSIS SANATORIUM

THE EASTBOURNE TUBERCULOSIS Sanatorium in 1914, situated near the bottom of East Dean Hill; you pass it when entering Eastbourne from Brighton on the A259. This photograph, taken shortly after the tuberculosis [TB] Sanatorium opened in July 1912, shows the whole hospital – and the postman. From the left are the two wards (male and female) of six two-bedded cubicles, with a nurse station in between. On the right, the administrative block and quarters for night nurses and other staff can be seen.

At the time, deaths from TB (or consumption) far exceeded those from cancer. The sanatorium was,

therefore, built at what was then the remote edge of the town because of the fear of infection. When reviewed, it was discovered that of the first 1,000 patients admitted 530 patients had died, and only 40 were well enough to return to work.

The windows of the patients' cubicles were kept open throughout the year to provide fresh air (notice that some of the beds are out on the verandas). The patients were well nourished to give them every chance of recovery, but there was no specific treatment. The isolation did, however, help to keep these infectious patients away from their families. This was particularly important for young children: in 1908, ten children were diagnosed with TB meningitis in Eastbourne; all died.

THE OLD SANATORIUM site, later Gildredge Hospital, became the Bodmin Close of today. From 1946, with the use of streptomycin and other new therapies, the number of tuberculosis cases and deaths plummeted. The first year with no recorded TB deaths in Eastbourne was 1968.

Gildredge Hospital (the name was changed in 1948 with the inception of the NHS) was utilised for other chest conditions, but it eventually outlived its usefulness and when the first phase of the King's Drive District General Hospital opened in 1976, all work transferred there. The Gildredge was razed to the ground in 1979: the land was sold, the receipts returned to the NHS and a new housing development, Bodmin Close, rose in its place.

DEVONSHIRE PARK

THIS PHOTOGRAPH SHOWS an era when bombs stopped play at Devonshire Park, famous for its tennis courts. The first tournament here was held in 1881 and now the Women's International Tennis Tournament, where the top stars prepare for Wimbledon, is an annual event. The ground caters for county matches and others organised by the Lawn Tennis Association throughout the season.

The area is low-lying, but the lawn tennis courts are second only to Wimbledon.

Saturday, 14 September 1940 was a day of repeated attacks on Britain and Eastbourne. In the course of one mid-afternoon raid, five 250kg bombs were dropped on the Devonshire Park tennis grounds, and were said to have proved two points: firstly, that bombs dropping into lush soft ground often do little damage; and second, that the Germans weren't good sports to desecrate the tennis courts.

THE DEVONSHIRE PARK public tennis courts in winter shadows. The main competitions take place in the International Lawn Tennis Centre courts. There are a few obvious differences – on the left skyline, for example, you can see the bulk of Devonshire Mansions, flats recently built on the site of the Devonshire Park Swimming Baths, and the exhibition hall – but in general the changes are slight. There are the more subtle changes, such as the replacement of glass in the roof and side panels of the Winter Garden with a tougher material even though it cuts down the light passing through.

When Wimbledon changed its turf a few years ago the grass was transferred to Eastbourne's championship courts.

BEACHY HEAD COMMEMORATIVE SEAT

EASTBOURNE TOWN AND pier can be seen on the right, some 2 miles away. This seat commemorated the Down's purchase, when Eastbourne County Borough, in what was their most statesman-like act, bought 4,000 acres (1,700 hectares) of Downland pasture on Beachy Head between 1926 and 1929 to save it from development, so that future generations could continue to enjoy this delightful spot. It cost an average of £22 an acre. Plaques set in a stone seat were unveiled in October 1929 by the Duke and Duchess of York – later, of course, King George VI and his consort Queen Elizabeth (the 'Queen Mum').

The seat looks solid enough, but is it overly ornate and does it appear somewhat out of place perched on the cliff top – or should that be 'over the top'?

THE 1929 SEAT was damaged by enemy action during the Second World War and removed from the site. This new seat, officially unveiled in November 1971 by the 11th Duke of Devonshire, represents a practical approach towards affording the visitor a seat to admire the view towards Eastbourne and Hastings whilst keeping out of the wind. This viewpoint is the same as for the 1929 seat, with the pier just visible on the right, but the seating is only on the leeward side. There are now many informative plaques here.

More recently the council has taken many measures to make the delights of Beachy Head's soft Downland turf, the fresh sea breezes and the wonderful views available to all visitors, and a path has been constructed to improve access for the disabled.

ARLINGTON ROAD

ARLINGTON ROAD AT the height of the air raids. On Thursday, 26 September 1940, just after 4 p.m., when the Battle of Britain was raging overhead, two aircraft attacked the town, damaging the railway station, St Leonards Road, Commercial Road, Old Orchard Road and here, Arlington Road, where a ruptured water main can be seen discharging in the centre of the road. Two unexploded bombs were also located, one of them going off four hours later.

The For Sale notice is understandable, but it would be surprising if many potential buyers turned up.

A MORE PEACEFUL prospect presents itself today, of a central residential area. This view is much tidier than seventy years ago (apart from the automobiles strewn everywhere). Even some of the trees have survived and there are no For Sale notices visible which could mean contented folk who can sleep in bed at night without worrying about a possible air raid.

LEWES OLD BANK, LATER BARCLAYS BANK

LEWES OLD BANK opened this branch in Eastbourne in 1896. It was later taken over by Barclays Bank.

On Sunday, 7 March 1943, just after noon, an assortment of fifteen Me 109s and FW 190s sped low, as usual, across the 60 miles of Channel and climbed over Beachy Head from where, after bombing a radar station, the formation raced across the town dropping bombs on Meads, Ocklynge cemetery, Cornfield Road, the Mostyn Hotel on the front and destroying three houses in Jevington Gardens. In Terminus Road Barclays Bank, along with Prings, the furnisher's, next door, took the full force of a 500kg bomb from an FW 190. Fourteen civilians were killed and over fifty injured.

THE BANK WAS effectively demolished by 8 March 1943. When the dust cleared, the bank's business was forced to continue from a small hut towards the left.

The replacement bank here, not quite so classical in concept, opened in 1958. The outside has had a few modifications over the last fifty years. The inside, however, has had several complete makeovers – with, for example, the broad, open counters reduced to queuing lanes and security screens.

This part of Terminus Road has been pedestrianised and the Arndale Centre, which opened in 1980, lies behind the bank.

ST MARY'S PARISH CHURCH

ST MARY'S PARISH church, Eastbourne, *c*.1880. This is the oldest church in the town and, for most of its history, the only one. Building of the church began in 1160 in a mixture of Caen stone (shipped over from France), Eastbourne greensand and chequered flint. In the 1300s the nave was extended and the tower added.

The bells that are heard today were first rung in October 1818. Extensive restorations were undertaken in the mid-1800s when the roofs were re-covered and the tower repaired.

There are many memorials to local families such as the Gilberts and Gildredges – and one to a Henry Lushington jnr who escaped the Black Hole of Calcutta!

APART FROM SOME street widening, not much has changed. Burials in the churchyard ceased in 1894, but there are interesting items such as memorials to the Brodie family and a Celtic cross given by the Gilberts. A porch was added to commemorate parishioners who lost their lives in the First World War and there was some minor damage in the Second World War, with one window blown out.

MARKS & SPENCER

EASTBOURNE'S MARKS & SPENCER shop in 1912. This Eastbourne shop opened on 27 July 1912 at 51 Terminus Road. Before the First World War you were expected to do your window shopping and only when you had decided what to buy did you enter the shop. Shops even employed youths to appear to window shop and comment how good or cheap the items were to entice people to enter. Essentially, 'the Admission Free' sign meant you were free to browse inside.

In 1937 the shop was extended to include number 53 Terminus Road.

SADLY, THE OLD shop was flattened in the 'Christmas bombing' of midday, 18 December 1942, when over fifty shoppers were killed or injured.

mainly women and children (including a boy of nine months and an eleven-year-old girl). The local Air-Raid Precautions teams were overwhelmed as they struggled to extricate those buried under a mountain of rubble, and the Home Guard and locally based Canadian troops were called in to help.

Temporary premises were used until, in May 1955, the store was able to reopen at the old site (although now renumbered Nos 133-137 Terminus Road). After a few relatively minor upgrades and modifications, this is what it looks like in 2012.

STATION PARADE

STATION PARADE IN the 1960s. Station Parade started as a line of single-storied buildings dealing with materials, such as coal, that came into Eastbourne by rail. The names on the fronts here were those of Bradford's, coal merchants, and Rickett's, similarly involved in coal and coke wares.

In 1911-12 these shack-like, 'just grew-up' buildings were swept away and the Station Parade of today was built, with many of the original retailers remaining. Bradford's, for example, had the shop just around the right-hand corner into the 1970s.

In the 1960s there was a wide range of retailers here, from Hall & Co., builders' merchants, to Oswald Field Ltd, a fashion retailer, and from A. Proctor and Son's dispensing chemists (still there today) to a branch of the Scotch Bakery (Sussex) Ltd. Louis G. Ford – owner of an eponymous builders' merchants and ironmongers – had been one of the original shop owners; he made his first sale, for goods worth 5*s*, in January 1912. Over the 1960s Louis G. Ford's premises gradually spread to encompass most of the shops here.

THE STRUCTURE NOW is exactly the same as shown above, albeit a little careworn. After Louis G. Ford's business was swallowed in turn by Graham's, locally based in Hammonds Drive, Station Parade reverted to hosting a variety of businesses: barber's shops, tanning salons and kebab takeaways in particular. Proctor's is there today, though now selling 'helps for everyday life' aimed particularly at the elderly and surgical products such as special shoes.

CHURCH PARADE, WESTERN LAWNS

CHURCH PARADE, WESTERN Lawns, *c*.1910. This was the scene after church on a Sunday morning when the elites among the visitors to Eastbourne and the locals paraded, exhibiting their finery while demonstrating that they could afford an army of servants and a cook to prepare their Sunday luncheon. It was also an occasion when the exquisitely finished belles and beaux could size each other up while their parents could assess their suitability. Those who didn't qualify to be included named it 'the Snoot Parade'.

Things were certainly different then in many ways. The Grand Hotel, just peeping in on the right and which continues as Eastbourne's five-star hotel, when opened in 1877 had only six bathrooms for 200 bedrooms. Mind you, a guest could request a maid to bring ewers of hot water to their room at any time of the day or night.

THE CHURCH PARADE which commenced in Victorian times lasted into the inter-war period in one form or another. Today the Lawns usually have a less crowded look and the Snoot Parade's numbers are only reached on special occasions such as the annual 'Airbourne' display.

One of the features is that the centre of the Lawns has a bronze and granite statue, erected in 1910, of the 8th Duke of Devonshire (1833-1908). He is represented wearing the robes of Chancellor of Cambridge University and holding a pince-nez in his hand, as was his habit. He had succeeded the Duke most associated with Eastbourne in 1891. The 8th Duke, who was a national figure, reduced his spending on the town and tended to put his money into shares rather than land, but he was the town's mayor in 1897-98.

His eminence didn't prevent the local lads, when celebrating a rugby victory or a wedding at the Grand, from clambering up the statue to place a chamber pot on the distinguished 8th Duke's head.

ROYAL SUSSEX REGIMENT MEMORIAL STATUE

ROYAL SUSSEX REGIMENT Memorial Statue in 1906. This memorial to those of the 2nd Battalion Royal Sussex Regiment who died on service between 1882 and 1902 was designed by Sir William Goscombe John, and the statue was unveiled by the Duke of Norfolk in 1906. Behind is Cavendish Place, in Regency style, with all the decorative hoods on the balconies in place.

Friedrich Engels, the close associate of Karl Marx, stayed in Cavendish Place during his regular holiday visits to the town and, in accordance with his wishes, in 1895 his ashes were scattered off Beachy Head. Marx also came to Eastbourne for holidays.

THE STATUE SEEMS to have come through over a century of observing the world go by without too much damage. Allowing for the inevitable change in car ownership, Cavendish Place, just by the pier and seafront, shows only a few modifications, with an occasional chimney pot and tree lost. Most of the balcony hoods remain in place and even the letter box is there, although it might have been moved a fraction.

LOOKING TOWARDS THE PIER

VIEW FROM THE Wish Tower towards the pier, *c*.1905. The water's edge shows plenty of bathing machines and a horse or two of those employed to pull them up and down the beach. The Birdcage bandstand is towards the right.

On the left there is the Mayfair Hotel, followed by Howard Square, the West Rocks and Sandhurst Hotels, and after Burlington Place the Cavendish Hotel – and then comes Devonshire Place, easily recognised.

The group of young ladies in white at the right lower margin have brought to mind wedding bridesmaids, or that they are coming from confirmation, or even Empire Day celebrations. A holiday on Empire Day commenced in 1902 and continued into the 1950s when it was renamed Commonwealth Day. The date was 24 May, Queen Victoria's birthday.

THE PHOTOGRAPH WAS taken in early spring with few holidaymakers about. Some chalets are seen and the 1935 central bandstand stands out on the right opposite Devonshire Place.

At the upper-left edge is the T & G Eastbourne Centre, opened in 1966, replacing the bomb site of the Mayfair Hotel, destroyed in the Second World War. Moving to the right (east), after Howard Square are the West Rocks and Albany Lions Hotels and after Burlington Place the tall Cavendish Hotel. The right (eastern) wing of the Cavendish has been rebuilt in a different style after losing an argument with a 250kg (500lb) German bomb on 4 May 1942. It was a legitimate target because it was being used as an RAF training school for navigators. It might have been to Germany's advantage to leave it, however, for one of those trained there admitted that whenever he calculated the position of Eastbourne he always seemed to put it in Hertfordshire.

THE WESTERN PARADES

THE WESTERN PARADES near Meads, *c.*1900. Bathchair parade seems to be the fashion. This is the third parade down by the sea and you can imagine that the sea has recently splashed up across the parade, for the height of the shingle protection is less and there were fewer groynes than today.

It was rumoured that the three layers of parades was decided upon in the 1880s to conform to the class structure of the day. Hence the lower orders could be accommodated on the lowest parade, while, naturally, the middle class clung to the central parade and the upper parade was the natural home for – well, most people are not so sure, because they've seldom been allowed there themselves.

HOW TIMES CHANGE! Not a bath chair in sight, thanks in part to artificial hips and knees, and being able to have your hip pinned if you happen to break the neck of your femur in a fall. Before pinning appeared in the 1920s, breaking a hip could be life-changing: if you broke your hip, in the vast majority of cases, you never walked again.

Apart from the health and safety railings on the right and the raised shingle and extra groynes, the parades themselves have hardly changed: even the thatched shelter is there on the left, partly hidden by bushes.

At the left edge is the end of the series of chalets, No. 2 of which (nearer Holywell) was visited by the King and Queen in March 1935.

EASTBOURNE PIER

THESE ENTRANCE KIOSKS were the original ones from the 1870s. This pier-head theatre opened on 15 July 1901; it had a 1,100 seat auditorium and boasted a Camera Obscura. That same year, the pier's first electric light was installed by Caffyn's. The games saloons halfway along the pier, built around the same time as the theatre, are clearly shown.

The junction of the pier, marking the point where the landward part was swept away in an 1877 storm, is not even: when it was reconnected, the landward piece was higher than the old remaining stretch. This difference in heights, it was stated at the time, was intentional.

The Carpet Gardens are to the right, with a row of bath chairs for hire along the left edge of the gardens.

A ferry boat is in view and probably has just left the pier – possibly on a day trip to France. While piers gave Victorians the chance to walk on water, their main purpose was to offer the chance of a sail.

THE PIER TODAY, looking south east. The pier has the 'new' entrance building dating from 1951. This replaced the 1912 kiosks. Just behind the entrance is the music pavilion, which was erected in 1925. There is no charge to walk on the pier.

The Carpet Gardens have lost their line of bath chairs for hire. Vehicles for hire were controlled by law, and in Eastbourne the council had laid down specific areas where waiting for hire was allowed. These were marked by metal licence plates. They are scattered round the town, not all in their original place, but may best be seen while you are on the front, particularly along the base of the stone wall bordering the extent of the Wish Tower's grounds and King Edward's Parade. They include a number of BCS (Bath Chair Stands), along with HCS (Hackney Carriage Stand) – and many others.

EASTBOURNE PIER CONTINUED

A VIEW OF the pier in 1912, here exhibiting its smart new kiosks; these lasted until 1951. In Eastbourne the kiosks did not open on Sundays until 1926.

P. & A. Campbell's paddle steamers, such as the *Brighton Queen* and *Devonia*, called regularly at the pier in the holiday season.

Between the wars the Clarkson Rose show *Twinkle* was the standard 'end-of-the-pier' show. In June 1940, however, an army detachment of sappers appeared with instructions to blow

up the pier – only to find that *Twinkle*, with an audience of 400, was in full swing at the end of the pier! The sappers were persuaded to wait until the final curtain, by which time the army had agreed not to blow up the pier, but to remove planking so as to completely inconvenience any invading Germans. If you walk on the pier today you walk on concrete slabs near the landward end, which, after the war, were used to fill the gap and lead on to the original wooden planking nearer the pier head.

AFTER THE WAR, the music pavilion of 1925 was converted into a ballroom, for at the time ballroom dancing had become popular. The pier theatre now offered summer shows, with Sandy Powell's *Starlight* running most years between 1948 and 1970.

In 1987 the theatre became the Roxy discotheque and Showbar. The old music pavilion became an amusement arcade, while there are shops at the entrance.

The original Eastbourne Pier Co. Ltd, one of the first limited companies, was registered on 3 April 1865 with £15,000 capital. The company sold out to Trust House in 1968/9 and Leisure Parcs paid £74 million for it in 1998.

The pier had a narrow squeak in 1963 when a ship on fire almost collided with it, and in 1970 an arsonist attempted to fire the theatre. It was saved, but access to the Camera Obscura was lost until 2004.

TERMINUS ROAD

THE STATION IS on the left, with a line of waiting horse-drawn taxicabs, and the station clock tower is just visible in this photograph from around 1900, though mainly hidden by the trees. The Gildredge Hotel is in the centre, and the shops on the right appear to be doing good business.

The roadway looks as though it had been recently watered to keep the dust down, for tarmacadam was not introduced into Eastbourne until 1911.

THE STATION HAS had many 'makeovers' in the intervening years, both inside and out, but the station

clock tower remains a feature, as does the renovated Gildredge Hotel just left of centre. Straight ahead in the distance is the part of Terminus Road, which forms the town's main bus station (popularly known as 'Diesel Alley').

There are a few remaining trees on the right, but the shops are in a sorry state, with boarded-up windows and even evidence of fire damage. The roadway, however, is cleanly marked and macadamed.

CONGRESS THEATRE

THE 1,600-SEAT Congress Theatre was opened in 1963 by Princess Margaret in the presence of Dame Flora Robson and Sir Arthur Bliss.

In 1955 Eastbourne Council had contemplated building a new conference and concert hall seaward of Wilmington Square. This would have meant knocking down the Wish Tower (Eastbourne's Martello Tower), but when the tower was listed a decision was made: the Indian

Pavilion in Devonshire Park was instead knocked down and replaced with this typical 1960s building. It had many of the qualities needed for its functions, but the acoustics were not entirely satisfactory and the needs of large conferences could not always be met, although measures were taken to improve the situation.

AT LEAST THE lampposts are in the same place, although the design has changed. The Congress Theatre, now a listed building, is currently undergoing extensive refurbishment, although the shows go on.

To the left, the corner house on the other side of College Road, which burnt down, has been replaced by an Eastbourne College Music Centre. Just peeping round the protective scaffolding over the left front of the theatre is the new Towner Art gallery.

THE BEACH

CRICKET ON THE beach on a sunny Edwardian day. It looks like a lovely day to be playing cricket on the beach, but is there some 'underhand' bowling going on here? The wickets are made up of three beach spades, while a spade is being used as a bat – and is that a helmet she is wearing? Who says there was no women's cricket in those days, eh?

In the centre background is the Alexandra Hotel on Grand Parade: notice the chimney pots and the single storey building to the right of the hotel.

THE SAME VIEW today. As it was a crisp but cold spring day the cricket was called off, but there is still one brave family on the shingle beach. The Alexandra Hotel is unchanged: though the chimney pots have disappeared from the other buildings, the Alexandra continues to sport every pot shown 100 years ago. Just to the right of the Hotel is the same one-storey building.

Further right is a new block of flats, Devonshire Mansions, replacing a couple of hotels and the Devonshire Park Baths.

If you enjoyed this book, you may also be interested in…

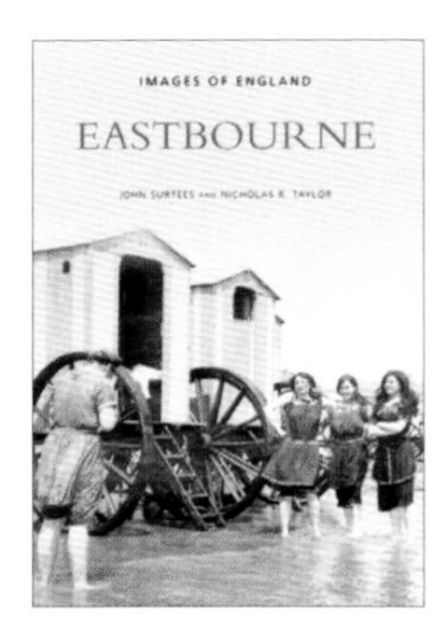

Eastbourne

JOHN SURTEES & NICHOLAS R. TAYLOR

This charming collection of over 240 photographs documents life in this thriving seaside town in the late nineteenth and twentieth centuries. All aspects of everyday life are recorded here, along with landmarks such as Eastbourne Pier, the Wish Tower and Beachy Head and events such as the moving of the Belle Tout lighthouse. *Eastbourne* will delight those who want to know more about the history of the town and evoke memories of a bygone time for those who have lived, worked or enjoyed a holiday here.

978 0 7524 3682 1

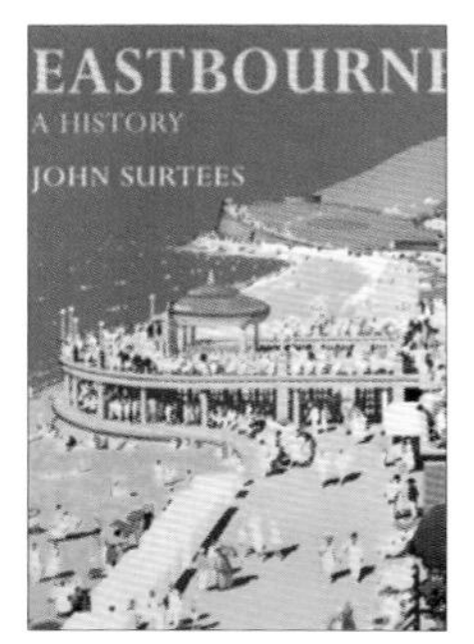

Eastbourne: A History

JOHN SURTEES

Eastbourne started as a fishing hamlet enlivened by the occasional bit of smuggling. The fashion for drinking seawater and sea-bathing was the principal catalyst for change, with the additional ingredients of the beauty of Beachy Head, the seal of a royal visit in 1780, the coming of the railway and the vision and support of the 7th Duke of Devonshire. Eventually, it became 'the Empress of Watering Places'. An entertaining and well illustrated account of the town's entire past.

978 1 8607 7226 9

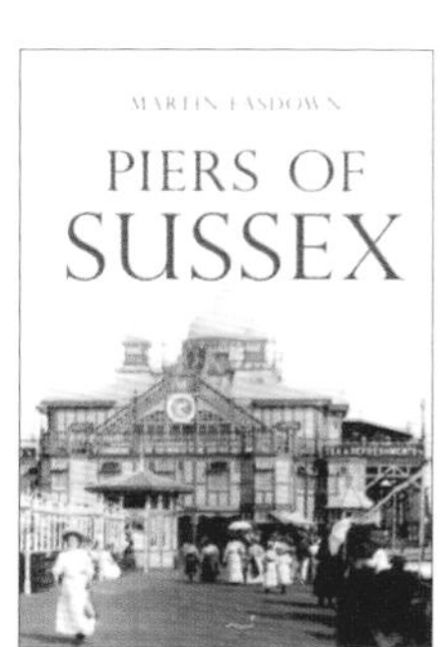

Piers of Sussex

MARTIN EASDOWN

Sussex has a good claim to be the birthplace of the seaside pleasure pier, for the famous Chain Pier at Brighton was the first to be used as a fashionable promenade. There followed a rich succession of piers, as from the 1860s until around 1910 as they were constructed in Brighton West, Worthing, Bognor, Hastings and Eastbourne. In their heyday they were the place to be seen. The county of Sussex should be proud to have retained six of its piers, including three of Britain's finest.

978 0 7524 4884 8

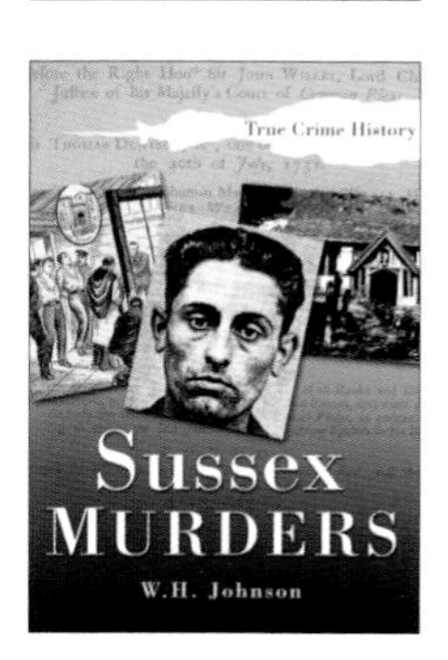

Sussex Murders

W.H. JOHNSON

Here is a look at the darker side of Sussex's history. Contained within the pages of this book are the stories behind some of the most notorious murders in Sussex's history. Based upon contemporary documents and illustrations, W.H. Johnson re-examines some of the crimes that shocked not only the county but Britain as a whole. All manner of murder and mystery is featured here, and this book is sure to be a must-read for true-crime enthusiasts everywhere.

978 0 7509 4127 3

Visit our website and discover thousands of other History Press books.

www.thehistorypress.co.uk